# INTRODUCTION TO APPRECIATION, MICROSOFT WORD, POWERPOINT AND, INTERNET UTILITY

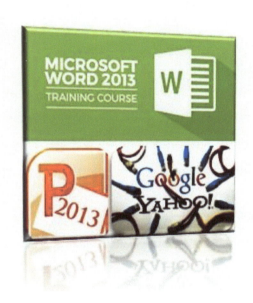

## BEGINNER –TO- ADVANCED

### BY

### WILLIE C.J.

# Table of Contents

# FORWARD

Learning how to use a computer is becoming a necessity in all fields of life. Barely will you get a profession presently that does not require basic computer knowledge for job placement. From the educational sector to the economy, church, institution, Government, etc. now depends heavily on Computers for the smooth running of their day to day operations.

The challenge is how to teach those that seek the knowledge as there is limited number of instructor in the ICT sector to serve the geometrically progressive audience who seek to learn computer. We indeed have enough teachers/lecturers in other fields of study but very few persons have gone into the ICT sector, making the demand for ICT instructors to be high. The ratio in a population of say 100 will be 100 students to 2 teachers.

Many rely on internet content, such as YouTube videos and instructional guide on websites. Unfortunately, some of these materials as good as they appear are still difficult for beginners to comprehend.

I was motivated by my student to write a book in this regard which will serve as an instructional material. This book can also be used as a self-tutor material. It covers the basic computer introductory courses and guides on how to use Microsoft Word 2013, PowerPoint 2013, and Internet Utility. I have carefully arranged the topics in a way that the student can easily flow from one module to another, the topics are arranged serially. In this book, I have not only taking out time to break down the steps on how to communicate this knowledge, but I have also added graphics for illustration and easy understanding.

The book is also backward compatible for those that are still using the old version of Microsoft Word below 2007, instructions on how to work with the older version of Ms. Word.

# Module 1

## Introduction to Computer

### What is a computer?

A computer is any machine or device which can accept data, process the data, and supply the results as information in a specified form.

In order words, a computer is an electronic device or machine which accepts data via the input device, processes it and sends the result via the output device.

### Computer Hardware

These are the physical components of the computer system that can be seen, touch and felt. They are divided into two parts, the input device and the output device.

**Input Device**

An input device is any piece of the computer hardware that is used in transferring data to the computer system. Examples are:

- **Keyboard:** It has a layout similar to that of a typewriter but has several extra keys, it is the most widely used input device. It allows the user to pass information to the computer, by typing in letters and commands on the keyboard.

- **Mouse:** A mouse is a hand operating device which is used to point and click items or command objects. A mouse is used with special programs which translate the mouse movements to corresponding actions on the screen. The mouse is useful in two ways. The first is to move the cursor on the screen and the second one is to select what you want the computer to do next.
- **Touch screen:** When it is touched, it senses where is touched, then the user can touch the exact task on the screen and the computer carries out the process.
- **Scanner:** This is also an input device that is used to scan documents or pictures into the computer.
- **Digital camera/ Phones:** These can accept the likes of pictures, audios, videos, etc. Phones can serve as both an input and an output device.

## Output Device

An output device is any piece of computer hardware that is used to retrieve information from the computer into a human-readable form. Example includes

- **Monitor:** It is a television-like display device which displays visuals on it. But actually, they work differently. It allows us to see the result of the work or command we gave the computer to perform on the screen.
- **Printers:** The printer takes the information stored on the computer and generate a hardcopy of the information.
- **Speakers:** It's an output device that allows the user to listen to sounds from the computer.

## Storage Components

The computer stores information using the storage device to hold information temporarily or permanently. The storage components are divided into memory devices and storage devices.

## Memory Device

The memory is divided into two parts namely the ROM (Read Only Memory) and RAM (Random Access Memory). RAM is used to store data temporarily before or during processing. RAM is a permanent storage unit that contains the instruction used for booting the computer.

## Storage Devices

It stores information on the computer permanently, and it can be recalled any time it is needed.

We have two types, the internal storage device example includes HARD DISK and external storage device example includes DISKETTE, FLASH DRIVE.

## Processor

Processor or Central Processing Unit acts as a "traffic warden" is the brain box of the computer. It has the capability to carry out logical and arithmetic instructions, interprets and executes program instructions, and communicates with the other components of the computer system.

## Computer Software

Software can be defined as a set of computer programs; instruction that causes the hardware to do work. Software as a whole can be divided into a number of categories based on the types of work done by programs. The two primary software categories are Systems software and Application software.

## System Software

They are usually written by computer software engineers and are directly responsible for ensuring optimal utilization of resources such as processor, memories, peripheral, etc. Their function is to make it easier to use application programs and hardware resources. Examples of system software are Operating systems (Windows, Linux, etc.).

## Application Software

These are programs designed for specific computer user application. They are produced by computer software engineers or programmers. Examples are; Word processing Ms. Word Creation, editing, formatting, and printing text, Spreadsheet Ms. Excel Performing mathematical and statistical calculation, Publishing PageMaker Creating and design of graphics.

Drawing and design Corel draw AutoCAD Design of image and structures.

## Computer Virus

A computer virus is a program written to alter the way computer operates without the permission or the knowledge of its owner. E.g. Jerusalem virus, worms, Trojans.

## Utility Software

These sets of software are used for maintaining, diagnosing and repairing the system.

### Antivirus

These are programs written to detect, remove and prevent computer viruses. An example includes Avira, Avast, Norton, McAfee Kaspersky, etc.

There is a need for precautionary motive in the handling of computer viruses, these are some of the motives to be taken.

➢ Know what files are stored on the hard drive
➢ Avoid inserting un-trusted storage device to be used on your computer
➢ Monitor the general and overall usage of your computer
➢ Always update your antivirus.
➢ Do not visit a website that is not trusted.
➢ Always scan the Graphic email attached to your mail before you open the file.

## Getting Started with Computer

**Booting and shutting down the Computer**
The process of loading the computer Operating system software to the desktop environment is referred to as booting. Press the power button in the system unit to initiate the booting process, also ensure that the monitor is turned on, the booting process may require extra input by the user to complete the booting process.

If the power to a computer is turned off before it is properly shut down, it could lead to loss of valuable data or damage to an open file. The proper steps to be taken when shutting down the computer is outlined below;

➢ Close all the open programs, before shutting down the computer.
➢ Open the start menu and click Shut down, or follow the arrow and click Shut down depending on the type of operating system being used.

## Desktop Environment

This is the background or home screen that is seen immediately after the booting process is completed.

**Features of the Desktop**

Windows desktop provides bars on the desktop to represent a collective group of features.

**Menu button** – It displays the menu such as user application and important system software that keeps the system running.

**The Task Bar** – This is found at the bottom of the desktop. It contains the start button, the Quick Launch toolbar and the taskbar tray (Which contains the clock and other icons.)

**Program Icons** - They are pictures that represent programs in a computer, they are mostly used in Windows application. They beautify the computer serves as shortcuts in launching an application.

## Using the Mouse and Keyboard

Mouse and Keyboard are integral part of the computer, which is used to position the cursor, enter text, navigate through documents, and enter commands and more. The Mouse has left and right button as well as the scroll button at the                                                   middle.

## Using the Mouse

Mouse and Keyboard are an example of an input device. The mouse especially requires some skills in using it. Some of its functions include:

**Clicking:** It simply means placing or pointing the cursor on an item such as text word paragraph, file, etc. and then pressing the left button and releasing it.

**Right-Clicking:** This is using the third finger to press the right button once, and a list of events that can be done comes out and then select it by                                                    clicking.

**Double Clicking:** This is the pressing of the left button at a very fast speed. It is used to open folders etc.

**Dragging:** It is a way of selecting an item and moving it away from its original position. It is done by holding the mouse down and holding the left button of the mouse.

Highlighting: It is also done the same way as dragging is done but it is used for text. It is used to select the text that wants to be edited.

**Using the Keyboard**

The keyboard primarily is used for entering text, symbols, punctuation, numbers etc. into the computer system. Apart from the function mentioned above the keyboard can also be used to perform special commands.

Mastering the keyboard and how to use it effectively requires dedication. For beginners, software such as Mavis Beacon and other typing tutorial application is a good tool to master how to use the keyboard. Some of this software is free and can be downloaded from the company's website for use.

## Starting a Program

Click the Start button or press the Window key from the keyboard Scroll or Click the "All Programs" then locate the program you want. Note if the arrow button shows, it means that it contains more program inside it.

**Create a program shortcut on the desktop**

1. Click start button
2. Scroll over the All Programs button and select the Application.
3. Right, Click and select send To Desktop.

**Opening a Document**

There are several ways to open documents in windows, these are:

**Opening a Document from within a Program**

1. On the File menu, click open.
2. To open a document in a different folder, click the arrow next to the look-in box, and then click the disk that contains the folder.
3. Click the folder that contains the document to be opened, and then click open. One may have to scroll to see more folders.
4. Click the document to be opened and then open.

**Opening a Document using the Document menu**

1. Click the start button, and then point to the document.
2. Click the name of the document to be opened
iii. The document opens, and a button for the document appears on the taskbar.

**Opening a Document using find command**

1. Click the start button and then on the start menu point to find or search.2. Double click its icon to open and then follow the proceedings.

## Features of the Window

An active rectangular part of the screen that contains a display different from the rest of the screen. Its features include:

**Title Bar –** It display the name of the program.

**The Status Bar** – This is found at the bottom of the window. It provides information about the current state of what is being viewed on the window and any other contextual information.

**The Toolbars** – It provides a quick way to access tasks. Most toolbar corresponds to a menu                                                  command.

**The Scroll bar** – If a window is not enough to display all the information, a scroll bar appears at the side (either vertically or horizontally) of the window. It can either be dragged or clicked.

**The Menu bar** – It is below the title bar, it displays an important menu like File, Edit, Insert, View, and Help, etc.

## Resizing a Window

One can reduce (minimize) or enlarge (maximize) programs and document windows to make work easier.

A window could be minimized to temporarily move it out of the way, but keep it active for later use .even so, a window could be maximized to see more of its contents on screen.

## Using Menu

A menu is a group of related commands that tells the window what to do. Many commands are organized in logical groups. For example, all the commands relating to starting a work in windows are on the start menu.

## Choosing menu commands Using mouse

1. Click on the menu title in the menu bar
2. Click a particular command of choice.

### Using Keyboard

1. Press Alt to activate the menu bar of the active window.
2. Use the arrow keys to highlight the menu title that is needed and then press the Enter button
or Press the key that corresponds to the underlined letter of the menu.

## Arranging Windows on the Desktop

1. Open multiple windows on the desktop, then point to a blank area on the taskbar and then Right click to reveal the shortcut menu.

2. From the shortcut menu, choose cascade to display the window in an orderly manner.
3. To display all open windows in equal sizes, Right-click the taskbar and choose Tile horizontal or Tile Vertically.

## Closing a Window

1. A window is closed by clicking the close (X) button at the upper right corner of the windows title bar.
2. Another way is by R Clicking on the window in the taskbar, then select close.
3. Another way us by pressing Alt F4 from the keyboard.

**Store documents into external storage device**

Insert the flash/removal device into its appropriate location.
1. Open the document to be transfer
2. Click the File or File icon on the tab menu.
3. Select Save As.
4. Browse to the location of the flash.
5. Click Save.

## Working with Files and Folders

## What is a File?

Files are defined as the collection of information with unique names. They are unique and cannot contain another file.

## What is a Folder?

A folder is a computer purse that is used to store data.

## Creating Folders

The reason for creating a folder is to store documents created so that document files will not be scattered among window program files.

## With window explorer

1. Open the start menu and choose Programs, then Windows Explorer.
2. Highlight the location for the new folder.
3. Select File New Folder. A folder icon named new folder appears at the bottom of the file list.
4. Rename the folder
5. Press Enter

## With My Computer

In My computer, open the icon or the folder in which the folder is to be created.

1. Select File, New. Windows create a new folder icon.
2. Type the name of the file and press Enter.

**From Desktop**
1. Right-click anywhere on the Desktop.
2. Select New, Folder.

**Deleting Folders**
1. Click on the folder to be deleted
2. Press Delete key on the keyboard
3. Click "Yes" on the dialog box that opens.

OR
1. Right, click on the folder.
2. Select Delete
3. Click "Yes" on the dialog box.

## Using the Recycle Bin

When Files or folders are deleted from the computer they are moved into the Recycle bin for which they can still be restored if the need arises. But once the Recycle bin itself has been emptied, the file or the folder cannot be recovered again.

**To Restore File or Folder**
1. Double click on the Recycle bin icon on the Desktop.

2. Right-click the file or the folder.

3. Select Restore.

**Emptying/Purging the Recycle bin**

1. Right-click on the Icon.

2. Select the Emptying Recycle bin.

## Installing / Un-Installing a Program

Installation means adding a particular program which is not on your computer to the computer for use. To install a program, these are the steps needed to be taken. Some programs autorun by themselves.

1. Insert the CD, Diskette, Flash, etc. that contains the program into its appropriate location.

2. Double click My Computer Icon.

3. Select and double click on the icon that represents the executable file in the storage device.

4. The application starts the installation.

5. Follow the Dialog boxes that appear as the installation progresses.

**Un-Installation** means removing a particular program from the computer. These are the steps involved in the process:

1. Click on the Start button.
2. Click on the Control Panel tab on the menu pop up or settings for windows 10.
3. Locate Program and Features button, then click.
4. All programs that are available on your system appears then double click on the program or Right-click.
5. Select uninstall.

## How to setup Account Username and Password

1. Click on the Start button
2. Click on the Control Panel tab on the menu pop up.
3. Locate the User account button, then double click.
4. Click on the task you want.

# MODULE 2

## Word Processor

Word processor can be defined as any windows application or program that helps us to perform our basic office task with great ease, these include: typing filling storing, printing, scanning, etc.

Examples of word processors include:

* ❖ Microsoft word (Ms-Word)
* ❖ Microsoft Excel
* ❖ PowerPoint
* ❖ Corel draw

### MICROSOFT WORD

Microsoft word is a word processor capable of providing options such as typing, editing, spell checking, formatting, setting, storing and Printing office documents where necessary.

### Starting Microsoft Word

When Microsoft Word is started, a new document window opens, ready to begin typing the document.

Start All Programs Microsoft Office Microsoft Word or Double Click on Microsoft Word Icon.

## Features of Microsoft word

Microsoft word has all the basic components of a window i.e. title bar, menu bar, scroll bars, command button; minimize, maximize and restore button. They function the same way as that of windows applications. The mouse or keyboard can be used to execute commands in Microsoft word in the same way as in other Windows applications. Microsoft word allows you to open nine documents at the same time (enabled if your computer has enough memory available).

The Microsoft word displays a set of command icons below and top of the screen in what is called the power bar. Microsoft word gives shortcut keys which are either single stroke key or series of keystrokes.

## Working with Basic Document Operation

Some certain features are most often used when we work frequently on Microsoft word, they include:

**How to Create Fresh Document**

We follow the steps below to create a fresh document in Ms. Word (Ctrl + N):

1) Click on the File menu
2) Click on New
3) Under general, click on Blank Document
4) Click on Ok

**Saving MS Word document**

There are two ways in which we can save a document in Ms. Word application they are the "Save As" and "Save".

**The "Save As" command**

This is used when we just want to save a document into a particular location and also to name it the name we want.

1. Click on the File tab or File Icon, and click Save As.

2. Select the format you want it to be saved.

3. Type the name you want ad click Save. We can also use the command F12.

**The "Save" Command (Ctrl + S)**

This is used to save the document frequently as it is been typed. It is mostly used for the existing documents.

1. Click on File tab and click Save
We can also use the command (Ctrl + S).

## Closing the MS Word Document

The Close command is used to close a file or document after use.
1. Click File on the Menu bar to display a drop-down list.
2. Select Exit from the drop-down list.

## Opening a Ms. Word Document (Ctrl + O)

The open command is used to open an existing file, folder or document. Other ways to achieve this task include:
1) Click the File tab or Icon from the Menu bar to display the menu list.
2) Click the Open option to display the Open dialog box.
3) Select the location of the Word document.
4) Press the Open button to open the document.

## Using the shortcut (Ctrl + O)

a) By pressing the key on the keyboard, it shows the dialog box.
b) Select the document you want.
c) Click on open.

## How to Quit Ms. Word (Ctrl + O)

Press Ctrl + W on the Keyboard, then the window is closed or,

a) Click file menu
b) Click on exit.

## FORMATTING TEXT

Formatting text is the act of adding a special outlook to the text, some of the formatting options include; bold, font color, underline, etc.

You need to highlight the text before any of the formatting options can be applied.

## Highlight a Text

1. Move the mouse pointer to the text.
2. Press and hold down the mouse button and drag it over the text. This will cause shading on the text.

## Underlining a Text

Underline simply mean placing a line under the text, we do that by following the steps:

1. Highlight the text.
2. Click on underline icon **U** on the standard bar.

N/B: to remove the underline, simply repeat the process of applying underlining.

**Font Size**
This is the size of text when typing a document, it ranges from 8 to 72 and above.

**The Font Colour Tool "A"**
This allows to change the color of our text, by giving option to choose from. It is usually located on the Draw toolbar.

**Changing the Font color of the text.**
Step
a) Highlight the text.
b) Click the arrow of the tool in the drawing toolbar to display the color palette.
c) Choose the new color from the popup menu.

**Font style Tools**
Some of the frequently used commands in Ms. Word are the Bold, Italics, and Underline tools.
**Bold Tool (Ctrl + B)**
1. Select the text you want to bold
2. Click on the Bold icon B in the formatting toolbar.

**Italic Tool (Ctrl + I)**
1. Select the text you want to change to italic form.

2. Click on the Italic icon I in the toolbar.

**Font Effects**

There are many effects that can be done to your text. Font effects make text to be more understanding and more presentable. Examples of effects include: Strikethrough, Superscript, Subscript, Engrave, Hidden, etc.

Press Ctrl + Shift + P at once and have the list. Select the effect you want.

## Text Alignment

Majorly we have four text alignment tool, they are ;

1. Left Alignment (Ctrl + L). It aligns text to the left.
2. Right Alignment (Ctrl + R) It aligns text to the right.
3. Center Alignment (Ctrl + E) It centralizes the text.
4. Justify (Ctrl + J) It aligns text to both left and right margin.

The text alignment tool is applied by first highlighting the text. Click on the Home Menu, under the Paragraph group, select any of the alignment options of your choice.

## Document Styles

The style option provides the user with different text formatting templates for arranging documents. Each style type such as Heading 1, Heading 2, Heading 3, Normal, etc., has a preformatted font type, size, text color etc. The unique property of these styles type is that it creates links that are further used in creating quick document pages such as the table of content etc.

Steps:

1. Place your cursor in the position the style will be applied.
2. Click on the Home menu.
3. From the Style group, select the style of your choice.

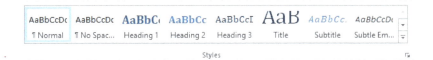

## Page Layout Menu

The margin, paper size and column are the major tools used in setting up a page.

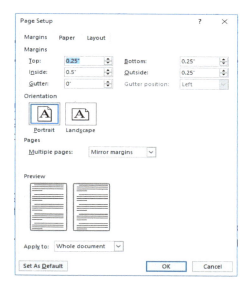

## Margins

The margins tab provides the option to set the margin of your document, the orientation of the paper to be used, preview setting and multiple pages option. It is better to leave the settings at its default otherwise, advance users can alter the settings.

## Paper Tab or Size

This tab gives us the option of selecting the size of the paper we want to use.

Steps:

a) Click on the file menu.

b) Click on the page set up arrow button.

c) Adjust the tool of your choice (margin, paper size etc.)

d) Click on ok.

For the 2007 version and above, click on Page Layout Menu. From the Page Setup Group select the tool of your choice, or click on the small arrow near the page setup group to access the page setup option.

## Working with Column

Columns are a special type of Ms. Word document type, it divides the page into column. Newspaper, hymn book and Bible are some of the examples of document type created with column.

Steps:

a) Place the cursor at the position where it will start.

b) Click on Format Menu for Office lower than 2007 version, or click on Page Layout for 2007 version and above.

c) Click on Column or drop-down arrow

d) Click on More Columns to display other options

e) Select your column style and indicate the number of columns.

f) Tick the box for Line Between (optional) if you want line to appear in the middle.

g) Click on the drop-down arrow in the **Apply To** section to select any of the options. Selecting the Whole Document option will apply the column to the entire page. Selecting the **This Point** **Forward;** will apply the column to only the section below.

h) Click on ok to apply.

## How to Apply Drop Cap

Drop Caps are used to indicate the beginning of a new story in a new document.

Steps:

a) Highlight the text.

b) Click on the Format menu for older version (OV) of Ms. Word. Click on Insert Menu for higher versions (HV).

c) Click on the box for Dropped (OV). Click on Drop Cap (HV).

d) Indicate the number of steps to drop (OV). Click on Drop Cap option and indicate the number of lines to drop, distance from the text, position and font type.

e) Click on ok.

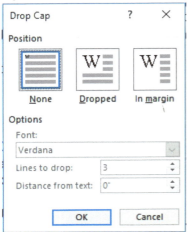

## Numbering and Bulleting

Steps:

a) Highlight the text you want to number or bullet.

b) Click on the Home Menu and select the numbering icon or bulleting icon.

c) For more option, click on the drop-down arrows to change the style of numbering or bulleting. You can also set a pre-defined numbering option from the more options drop-down list by clicking on the Define New (Number format, bullet, listing style).

## Tables

Tables are tabular work in Microsoft Word, you can create a table by using any of the three methods:

**Insert Table**

We can choose preformatted tables from the sample provided by selecting the number of rows and columns that we want (this option is only available in higher versions of Ms. Word).

Steps:

Click on the Insert menu, from the Tables group click on Table, select the number of rows and column.

**Table Templates**

You can use table templates to insert a table that is based on a gallery of preformatted tables. Table templates contain sample data to help you visualize what the table will look like when you add your data.

1. Click where you want to insert a table.

2. On the Insert tab, in the Tables group, click Table, point to Quick Tables and then click the template that you want.

3. Replace the data in the template with the data that you want.

## Table Menu

1. Click where you want to insert a table.

2. On the Insert tab, in the Tables group, click Table, and then, under Insert Table, drag to select the number of rows and columns that you want.

## Insert Table Command

You can use the Insert Table command to choose the table rows and columns before you insert the table into a document.

1. Click where you want to insert a table.

2. On the Insert tab, in the Tables group, click Table, and then click Insert Table.

3. Under Table size, enter the number of columns and rows.

4. Under AutoFit behavior, choose options to adjust the table size.

## Draw a Table

You can draw a complex table — for example, one that contains cells of different heights or a varying number of columns per row.

1. Click where you want to create the table.

2. On the Insert tab, in the Tables group, click Table, and then click Draw Table. The pointer changes to a pencil.

3. To define the outer table boundaries, draw a rectangle. Then draw the column lines and row lines inside the rectangle.

4. To erase a line or block of lines, under Table Tools, on the Design tab, in the Draw Borders group, click Eraser.

5. Click the line that you want to erase. To erase the entire table, see Delete a table.

6. When you finish drawing the table, click on a cell and start typing or insert a graphic.

## Convert Text to Table

1. Insert separator characters — such as commas or tabs — to indicate where you want to divide the text into columns. Use paragraph marks to indicate where you want to begin a new row.

For example, in a list with two words on a line, insert a comma or a tab after the first word to create a table.

### Two-column Table.

2. Select the text that you want to convert.

3. On the Insert tab, in the Tables group, click Table, and then click Convert Text to Table.

4. In the Convert Text to a Table dialog box, under Separate text at, click the option for the separator character that you used in the text. Select any other options that you want. Add or delete rows or columns

### Add Row Above or Below

1. Right-click in a cell above or below where you want to add a row.

2. On the shortcut menu, point to Insert, and then click Insert Rows Above or Insert Rows Below.

 NOTE    You can quickly add a row at the end of a table by clicking on the lower-right cell and then pressing

TAB.

**Add a Column to the Left or Right**

1. Right-click in a cell to the left or to the right of where you want to add a column.

2. On the shortcut menu, point to Insert, and then click Insert Columns to the Left or Insert Columns to the Right.

**Merge Table Row or Column**

1. Select the cells (rows or columns). From the Table Tools click on "Layout".

2. Click on merge cells from the Merge group

**Split Cell**

1. Insert the cursor to the position where you want the splitting to occur, or select the entire row.

2. From the Table Tools click on "Layout".

3. Click on Split cells from the Merge group.

4. Enter the number of rows or columns.

5. Click ok.

**Split Table**

1. Insert the cursor to the position where you want the splitting to occur, or select the entire row.

2. From the Table Tools click on "Layout".

3. Click on Split Table from the Merge group.

4. Click ok.

**Delete Table Row**

1. On the Home tab, in the Paragraph group, click Show/Hide.

2. Select the row that you want to delete by clicking to the left of the row.

3. Right-click, and then click Delete Rows on the shortcut menu.

**Delete Table Column**

1. On the Home tab, in the Paragraph group, click Show/Hide.

2. Select the column that you want to delete by clicking the column's top gridline or border.

3. Right-click, and then click Delete Columns on the shortcut menu.

### Delete the entire Table

1. Select the table you want to delete.
2. Click on Layout from Table Tools.
3. Click on the Delete tab and select Delete Table.

### Delete the contents of the Table.

You can delete the contents of a cell, a row, a column, or the whole table. When you delete the contents of a table, the table's rows and columns remain in your document.

1. Select the contents that you want to clear.

2. Press delete or Backspace button to clear content.

## Delete the content of a Row(s)/Column(s)

1. Click to the left of the row of a column(s).

2. Click the column's top gridline or border of a cell or click the left edge of the cell.

3. Press DELETE.

## Working with Graphics

Graphics can be imported into MS Word documents. The following steps explain how to import pictures to Ms Word:

1. Place the cursor to where the graphics are to be placed.

2. Click on the Insert menu on the Menu bar.

3. Scroll or click the picture tab.

4. Browse to the picture you want.

5. Click Ok.

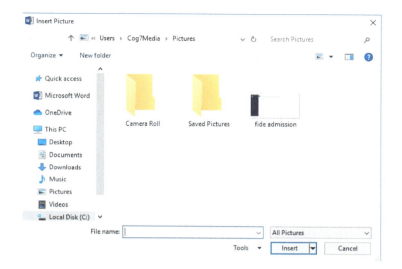

## Inserting picture from scanner or camera using the insert menu

1. Place the cursor to where the graphics are to be inserted.

2. Click on the Insert menu on the Menu bar 3. Under the illustration group, scroll or click the picture tab.

4. Select scanner and camera option from the menu list select the device you want to get the image from using the device name list.

1. Select an image from the device.

2. Click ok.

## Adding Auto-shape, SmartArt, and Chart to Ms. Word using insert menu

These diagrams aid in illustration and saves the users time in drawing a new object. The object can be modified to suit the demand of the user.

Steps:

1. Place your cursor to the position where you want to insert the chart.

2. Click on insert menu.

3. Under illustration group, select SmartArt, Shape or Chat tab.

4. Select the diagram type and click OK.

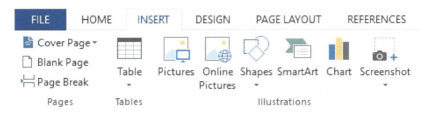

## Inserting Header and Footer

Steps on how to insert header and footer;

1. Click on the insert menu

2. Select the Header or the Footer icon from the Header & Footer group.
3. Select the Built-in option of your choice.
4. Enter your text and click on the close header and footer.

## Printing MS Word Document (Ctrl + P)

1. To print a document, click on the File tab or Icon.
2. Select a Print option on the menu list.
3. Select the printer to be used.
4. Specify the range to which it should be printed (All or Current page).

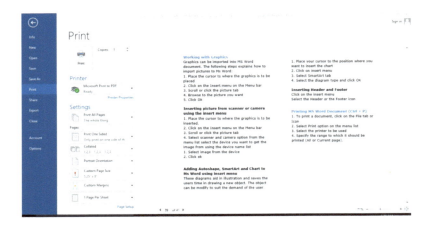

## Reference Menu

The Reference menu provides options for adding a book, journals and project reference features such as table of content, citation and the APA style of referencing.

**Table of Content**

Ms. Word 2007 version and above comes with inbuilt templates that make it easier to insert a table of reference.

This option only works when you adopt the Ms Word style of formatting document (i.e. heading 1, heading 2, Title, Subtitle, Normal, etc.). The table is generated based on the style of heading chosen.

Steps:
1. Place the cursor where you want to position the table of content.
2. Click on the References menu.
3. Select the Table of Contents tab.
4. Choose the table of the content type of your choice and click to apply.

## Citation and Bibliography

You can cite resource material and also generate a reference/bibliography page.

Steps:
1. Click on the Insert Citation tab
2. Click on Add new source and fill in the option provided accordingly.
3. Click on ok to apply.

## Insert References/Bibliography

Steps:
1. Click on References menu
2. Select Bibliography from the Citation and Bibliography group.
3. Select Reference or Bibliography from the drop-down list.

## Design Menu

The design menu is only available in Ms. Word version 2013 and above. It has some interesting features in its list such as page theme and style, watermark, page color, and page borders.

## Watermark

Watermark features are used for checkmating copyright piracy and also to show the authenticity of a document.

Steps:

1. Click on the Design menu.

2. Select watermark from the page background group.

3. Click on the watermark style of your choice to apply.

You can also create a custom watermark by adding custom text or using a picture by clicking on the custom watermark and follow the instructions on the dialog box.

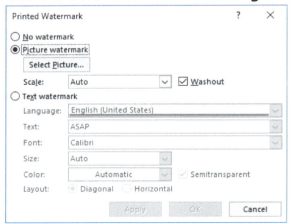

## Page Color/Border

The background of the page is usually white by default, but certain designs may require changing the background to a custom color.

Steps:

1. Click on the Design menu
2. Select page color from the page background group.
3. Select the color of your choice from the drop-down list.

Similarly, we can also add effects such as page border to our page.

Steps:

1. Click on the Design menu
2. Select page border from the page background group.
3. From the dialog box, select the page border tab and follow the instructions.
4. Click on ok to apply.

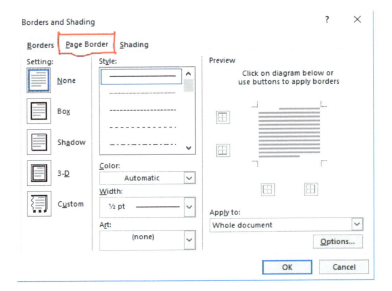

## Document Formatting Tool

The tool comes with pre-formatted themes and designs to format our document. This is similar to the Document style formatting in the Home menu.

Steps:

1. Click on the Design menu

2. Select Themes/Formatting Style from the Document Formatting group.

3. Select the theme/design of your choice from the drop-down list.

# Module 3

## POWERPOINT

### What is PowerPoint?

PowerPoint is an application basically used for creating presentations and illustrations. The presentations or illustrations are a collection of slides constructed from pictures, drawing, text, and clipart.

### PowerPoint Ribbon

The Menu bar which will be referred to as Ribbon in Micro Soft PowerPoint 2007 version and above is a collection of buttons across the top of the main window. The Ribbon enables the users can to navigate from one menu to another, it also provides access to anything the program has to offer.

### Create a New Presentation (Ctrl+N)

1. Select "File" then "New"

## 2. Click on the Blank Presentation to create a blank presentation.

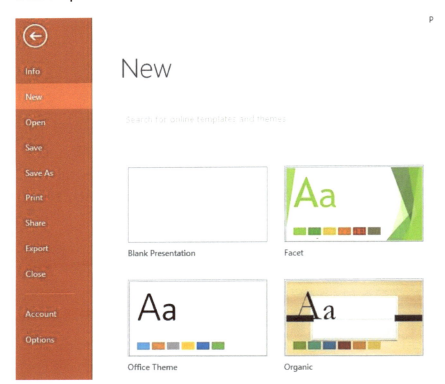

---

## Open an Existing Presentation (Ctrl +O)

1. Select "File" then "Open"

2. Navigate (Browse) to the location of the file, select the file and click on Open.

## Saving a Presentation (Ctrl + S)

- Select "File" then "Save As"

- Chose a location to save the file, and click on save.

## Create a Slide (Ctrl+M)

- Click the "Home" ribbon and select the "New Slide" button

- Select the Slide Pane and click on any slide template of your choice.

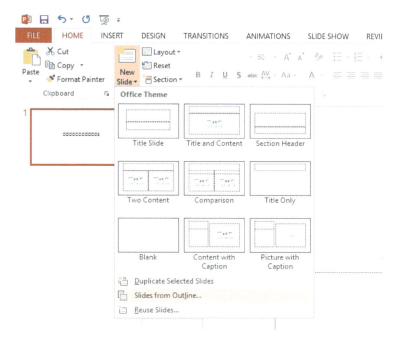

## Insert Picture from File

- Click the "Insert" ribbon then select "Picture"

- Navigate to the image file from the folder to where it is saved.

- Select the picture and click on "Insert" from the dialog box.

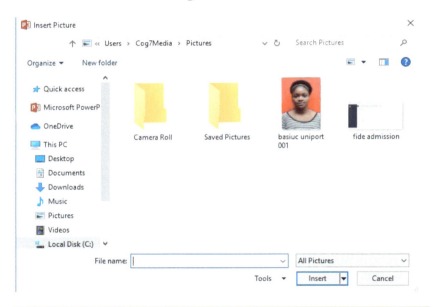

## Insert Shapes

- Click the "Insert" ribbon then select "Shapes"

- Select the shape of your choice.

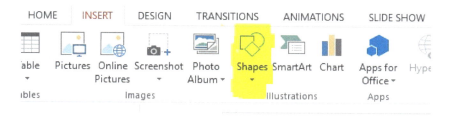

## Format Picture

- To resize the image, click on the picture to surround the image with a blue box.

- Drag the corner dot away from the center to make it larger and toward the center to make it smaller.

## Format Font Size and Style

Formatting fonts adopt the same method of operation in Ms Word.

- Click the "Home" ribbon then make changes to the font size and style of the text.

- This Home tab also allows you to change all aspects of the font size and style.

## Insert Header and Footer

- Click "Insert" then "Header and Footer drop-down"

- This dialog box allows you to add a date and time on the slide.

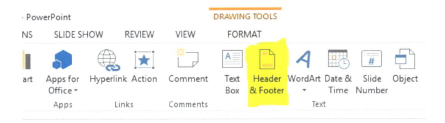

## Insert Hyperlink

- Click the "Insert" ribbon then hover over "Links" then select "Hyperlink"

- Select the "Link to option"

- Copy and Paste the Link from the website into the "Link" box.

- Click on ok

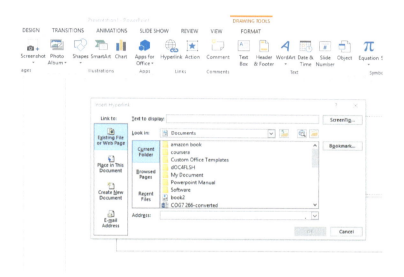

## Working with Tables

- Click the "Insert" ribbon then select "Table"

- Move the mouse over the table illustration to select the number of columns and rows of the table you would like to use.

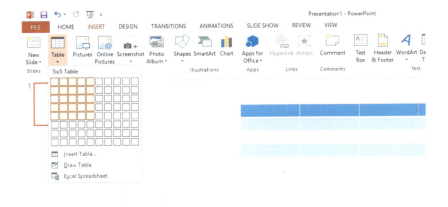

## Insert Charts

- Click the "Insert" ribbon then select the "Chart" button.

- Click Chart Option to choose from Area, Bar, Line, Pie and several other Chart Options.

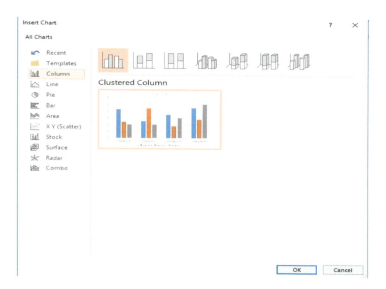

# Add a Slide Theme

- Click the "Design" ribbon

- Select a design theme from the Theme toolbar.

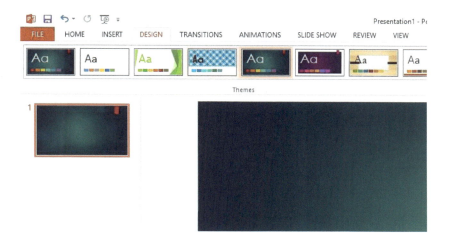

## Add Slide Transitions

- Click the "Transitions" ribbon

- Select desired Transition from toolbar

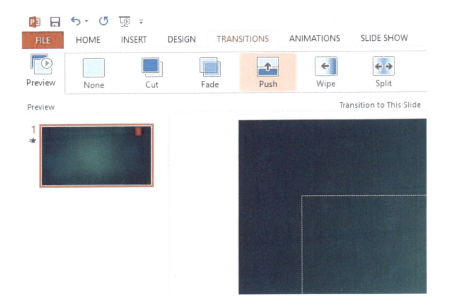

## Rearrange Slides

- To reposition a slide, click on the slide thumbnail in the left column

- Drag and drop the slide at the desired location.

- To reposition consecutive slides at one time, click and hold the Shift key to select the slides you want to move.

- Drag and drop the slides at the desired location.

## Preview a Presentation (Fn +F5)

- Click the "Slide Show" ribbon

- Select the point in the slide show that you would like to begin viewing (From beginning or From current slide)

## Presentation Views

- Slides in a presentation can be viewed and edited in different ways. This can be selected from the View menu.

- The Normal view is the default view can only show one slide per page.

- The Outline view is similar to the normal view, slides are shown as outline notes.

- Slide sorter view displays the entire slide available in a given presentation in one page. Users can easily sort and rearrange slides in this view.

- Reading view to preview the slides in full screen.

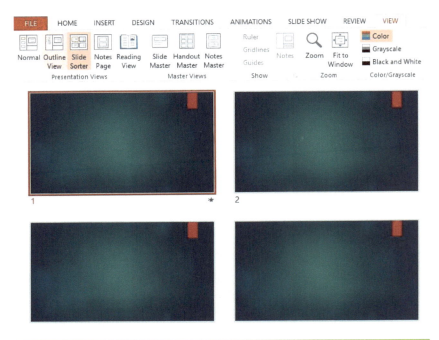

## Print Slide

- Click on the "File" then select "Print"

- From the dialog box select the printer and chose the document settings.

- Click on "Print".

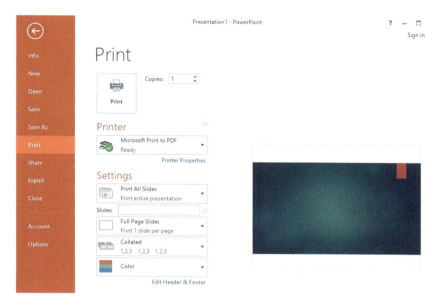

# Module 4

## Internet Utility

The application software for browsing (accessing) the internet is called browser. We have different types of browsers such as Google Chrome, Safari, Internet Explorer, Firefox, etc. Basically, they all do the same thing, the difference is only in the browser features, and some have more advanced features than the others. We are going to discuss how we can access the internet with browsers, download files, visit websites etc.

## Google Chrome

Google chrome is one of the easy to use browsers and comes with lots of features. It has a search engine option as the home screen.

## Basic Features

Title Bar: Displays the name of the webpage opened.

Address Bar: The address bar is used for typing website address (URL) e.g. www.gmail.com.

Navigation arrows (← →): The navigation arrows are used for moving back and forward. You can go back to a previous page by clicking on the ← button.

Reload button: Just as the name implies, for reloading a web page.

## Internet Explorer or Edge

Internet Explorer is the default browser for computers that run on Windows Operating system. The advanced form of it is the Edge application which is found in window 10.

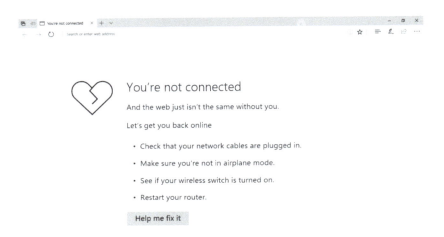

## How to visit a website

First, you need a browser. Open any browser of your choice and follow the steps below;

1. Type the address (URL) in the address bar e.g. "www.google.com"

2. Press the enter button from keyboard or click on Go, Ok Search button depending on the browser you are using.

## Downloading File

Downloading files from the internet is simple but can get complicated depending on the website you are pulling the file from. I am going to use a very simple example to show how you can download files online.

These are some of the website where you can download files;

Software: www.filehippo.com

Movie: www.moviesmobile.net

Picture: www.pixbay.com

The following steps explain how to download

## Search Engine

Search engines are web applications designed to carry out a web search. Google search (www.google.com) is one of the most popular search engines others include; ask.com, monkey.com, bing.com, etc.

Q Search Google or type a URL

## Watch Video/Music online

Youtube (www.youtube.com) is one of the largest video sharing website. There is another website where you can watch videos online such as www.divxcrawler.com (stream or download movies online), udemy.com, etc.

Steps:

1. Visit youtube.com

2. In the search bar enter the title of the video of your choice

3. Click to play video.

## How to Create an Email Account

Email address is one of the oldest means of communication since the inception of the internet. Sharing of files from one person to another is made possible via mail. The services are provided by different email hosting companies such as Gmail, yahoo mail, rocket mail, etc.

Creating an email account follows a different method depending on the company hosting the email. Generally, they all require the same type of information, although some may request additional information to create an account.

## Creating a Gmail Account:

Steps:

1. Visit the website www.gmail.com, or browse through Google and type Gmail to go to the account creation webpage.

2. Click on Sign in.

3. From the login page, click on don't have an account option to create a new account. Select the Create Account link and select any of the option. (Myself: to create a personal account and Business: to create a business account).

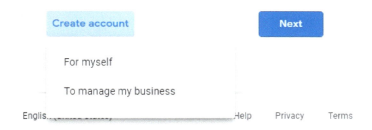

4. Fill in the information required in the form and proceed to the next page. You will be required to choose a unique email address and

password or you can also use the suggestions made.

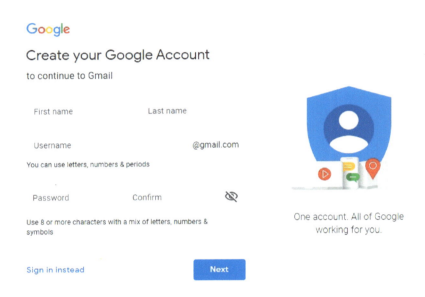

5. You will be required to verify the account with a phone number. Enter a valid phone number and proceed. Copy the verification code and enter the code in the space provided.

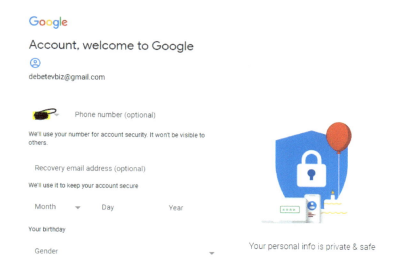

6. Accept the terms and condition to complete the process. A welcome page bearing your new email address will appear.

.